YOU

A TEENAGE
SOCCER REFEREE

Word Association Publishers
205 Fifth Avenue
Tarentum, Pennsylvania 15084
www.wordassociation.com
1.800.827.7903

ISBN: 978-1-63385-454-3

Library of Congress Control Number: 2022901602

Photo Credits:
Thanks to Katie Highsmith, Christian Rivas and Andrew Smith and their
families for providing me with the photos used on the front cover. Thanks also to
Matt Glass for letting me use his photo on the front as well.

The photos on the back cover were taken by my brother, Dan Glass,
who is not only an excellent photographer, but also a great referee as well.
I enjoy working games with Dan. His work can be found
at the Daniel Glass Photography website, DanGlassPhoto.com

A GUIDE TO SUCCESS

when, for the first time in your life an adult who is not your parent, teacher or coach is screaming that you don't know what you are doing.

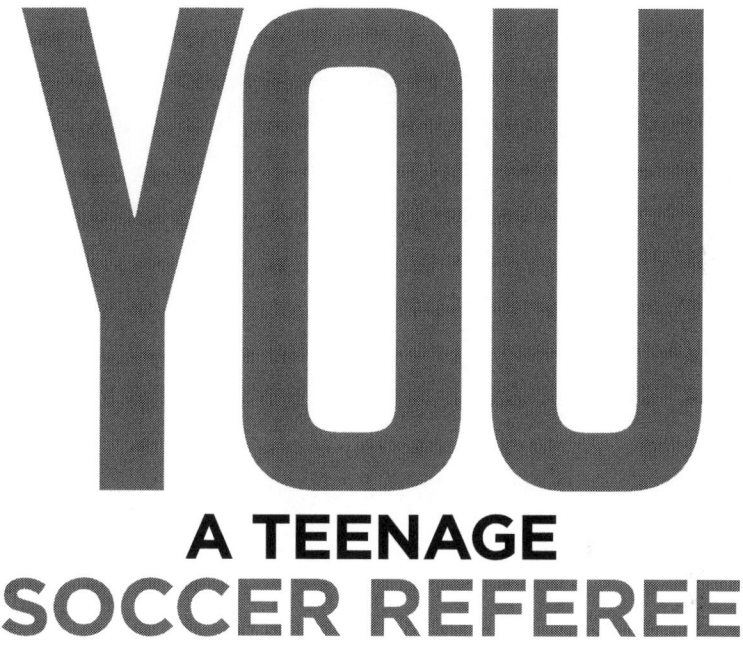

YOU

A TEENAGE
SOCCER REFEREE

BEN GLASS

WORD ASSOCIATION PUBLISHERS
www.wordassociation.com
1.800.827.7903

Organizations wishing to purchase this book in bulk
should go to *TeenageSoccerReferee.com*
for information and to order

CONTENTS

DEDICATION

I dedicate this book to my wife, Sandi who for over forty years has helped me balance my love for soccer refereeing with my responsibilities to family. This has not always been easy, trust me. Sandi has taught me the value of playing the long game "for the good of the game."

I also want to give a shout-out to all those teenage referees who are brave enough to at least give refereeing a try. You are doing what 99.99 percent of people will never do: put yourself out there to do something you believe is worthwhile while subjecting yourself to the judgment of others. Always remember this: The folks yelling at you from the sidelines would not have the courage to do what you're doing. The soccer community thanks you for giving refereeing a try.

A BRIEF DISCLAIMER AND WHY YOU SHOULD LISTEN TO ANYTHING BEN GLASS HAS TO SAY ABOUT REFEREEING

As you will read, I first picked up a whistle and began refereeing on the dusty fields of Annandale, Virginia, when I was sixteen. I'm still at it at age sixty-four, and my goal is to one day be "that guy" on a YouTube video titled "The oldest soccer referee and look how good he looks!"

Today, I am what US soccer calls a grassroots referee. When I was younger, and before I took a break from refereeing to start a family and begin my legal career, I was a state referee.

That means I've reffed lots of games. Lots, from herding a bunch of five-year-olds to many very "interesting" adult games (where many players acted like five-year-olds) in the ethnic leagues that abounded in the Washington, DC, area in the '70s and '80s.

While playing soccer at William & Mary, I got to just about every public and private high school field in the Tidewater area. Today, my time is split between boys' and girls' high school games and the youth leagues in Northern Virginia.

No one "certified" me to write a book for youth referees. I don't have a fancy badge, nor am I an instructor. I'm just a dad of nine running two highly successful businesses who still gets an andrenaline rush and a nervous feeling when I go out to do a game, any game, and I'm putting my ideas about refereeing, particularly the teenage soccer referee experience, out into the universe for you to consider.

I do have a ton of experience managing the people involved in soccer—the players, coaches, spectators, and my fellow referees who are taking the field with me to this day. I have thought deeply about the issue of a ref's proper mindset when it comes to refereeing soccer games, and I'm sharing those thoughts with you in this book.

I think the game is in danger. A minority of adults in the youth game are making it miserable for the referees, the coaches, and yes, their own kids.

Please just stop it.

Let kids play.

This book is for teenagers who look at refereeing and say, "Know what? I'd like to try that," but when they stop to think about it, they remember that minority of adults who are out to ruin youth soccer, and they hesitate about putting themselves out there to potentially face abuse.

Please stop it if you are one of "those" adults and you happen to be reading this book. If you are a responsible adult and have "one of those parents" on your kid's team, do what I did when my kids were playing: Tell those adults to shut up.

I have invited two of my refereeing friends, Eric Highsmith and Jesse Rosenthal, to contribute their thoughts here as well. You will find their bios in the back of the book.

One more thing as we begin. I'm putting my ideas out there just like young referees put themselves out there when they step onto a field. I recognize that there will be those who don't agree with every word I write.

That's okay. I get it. Write your own book, and I'll read it!

FOREWORD

I started as a little chubby six-year-old playing soccer with my local club when I developed my love and passion for the beautiful game. Years later, I realized I wasn't good enough to become a professional player, but I still wanted to stay close to the game. That's when one of my teammates suggested I become a referee, and I loved it.

Along my journey, I met many great people such as Ben, who stands out among the rest with his extensive refereeing knowledge and experience. I learned a lot of things from Ben but most important to enjoy refereeing, and I want you to enjoy it as well.

Let me take you back to when I first started refereeing soccer as a skinny fourteen-year-old with an oversized yellow referee shirt walking to the field where I would take charge of a boys' U-8 match. Before the match, I was a nervous wreck, but I went, spoke to the coaches, who seemed sympathetic with me, and blew my first-ever whistle. There were a few things I wish I knew back then that I know now including, What the hell do I do with this forty-year-old man who's yelling at me in front of all these kids?

This book will help you answer that and a lot of other things you'll want to know before going into your first few matches. It's something I wish I could have read before I started refereeing. I mean, who better to give you advice for your first few matches than Ben Glass, who has been a soccer referee for almost fifty years? It'll help prepare you to get out on that field and be confident because—trust me—refereeing is one of those things where you sometimes need to "fake it till you make it."

If you're reading this, you're probably an ambitious person. I'm not trying to scare you, but it will get tough sometimes as is the case with all professions. Don't get discouraged because you had in the words of Brian Barlow—USSF and NISOA Referee—"a bad cheeseburger who tried to ruin the game." Just know you're going to make mistakes and that's okay! You're following the footsteps of many of the greats such as Pierluigi Collina and Howard Webb, and now it's your turn to write your history.

— Christian Rivas,
teenage soccer referee and creator of RefNext.org

INTRODUCTION

"LET'S BEGIN A BOOK ABOUT SOCCER REFEREEING WITH AN UMPIRE STORY"

I have nine children, and they played a variety of sports growing up including soccer, baseball, football, basketball, field hockey, and lacrosse. As you can imagine, I ended up attending and coaching a *lot* of games including Little League baseball games.

Over the years, I learned that it was common for a game to be short an umpire. I would sometimes volunteer to help out; the teams usually needed someone just to watch first base. That was pretty easy; the only thing I really had to rule on was whether a runner was safe or out.

On one memorable day, however, no umpire showed up at all. If they couldn't find a volunteer to get behind the plate, the game would probably have been cancelled. This job wasn't as simple as watching first base. This person would have to put on the equipment and take a place *behind the catcher*. But

I had watched many games from the stands and the dugout. *How hard could this* be? I asked myself.

I had, after all, decades of experience as a soccer referee. In those games, I commonly ran two, four, five, six miles a game tracking lots of action all at once on a very large field and had dealt with crazy coaches and parents. In Little League, you just stand behind the plate, the ball comes to you, and you make a simple decision! *I just have to figure out whether that ball crossed the plate above the batter's knees and below his armpits*, I told myself. *Easy-peasy. I've been judging pitches from the stands for years and never missed one!*

Right.

Maybe I should have taken a moment to think about my few experiences as a youth basketball referee when I was in high school. I was good at soccer; it made sense to me, so refereeing soccer games felt natural. But I was not a "basketball guy." I had played some but not at a very high level. On the court, I learned that it was one thing to read the rules, take a class, and pass a test, and it was another to develop a real feel for the customs and culture of the game. Add to that the fact that basketball referees run around with whistles in their mouths rather than holding them as they do in soccer. I can't tell you how many times I blew the whistle for a basketball foul before my brain was fully in gear and got myself into trouble.

Stand behind the plate? No problem. I raised my hand and announced, "I'll ump the game." What can I say? My heart was in the right place. I wanted those kids to get to play. I was nervous ... so nervous that I forgot to pick up the big chest protector that Little League umpires hold like shields in front of them. (Experienced umpires have special vests they wear under their shirts, which looks a lot cooler than hugging a big blue pillow for a whole game.) At least I knew enough to put on a mask! (Later, you will read about a soccer referee who wore shin guards to his first game because he thought he was supposed to dress just like the players.)

About four pitches into the game, the young catcher (probably playing his first game as catcher) missed a high, hard fastball that zinged off my shoulder. Yikes! That hurt! "Hey ump!" someone yelled from the stands. "That's what the chest protector's for!"

Slightly embarrassed, I waved nonchalantly, called a time-out, and headed back to the umpire storage shed.

When the game resumed, I began to see that this job was different from soccer. Soccer referees can be out there and think they've seen a foul but then wonder if they were correct. If in doubt, soccer refs will sometimes yell, "Play on!" It's the sports equivalent of "Move along folks ... Nothing to see here."

But you can't do that in baseball. When players wielding aluminum bats swing, they either miss or connect. Miss and it's a strike. Connect and foul, it's a strike (at least the first two times). Connect and hit it over the shortstop's head, it's a fair ball. But if they *don't* swing, the umpire has to make a decision—ball or strike. Very binary. They must then publicly announce their decision on every pitch the batter doesn't swing at.

There I was crouched behind home plate. My heart was racing. My eyes and brain just didn't seem to want to synchronize. I realized, *Oh my gosh, I have about half a second, maybe a full second, to make a decision about whether the ball was too high or too low or outside or inside!* It had always looked so easy from the stands. Half the time, before my brain could analyze what I had just seen, my eyes convinced my voice to yell, "Strike!" Then half a second later as the young pitcher would look at his coach with that *Where did we get this guy?* look, my brain would tell me, *No, that wasn't a strike. Way up high.*

I'll get it right next time! I would promise myself. I was doing my best, and the coaches and players were tolerating me. But after a couple of innings, I started hearing mumbling from the dugout: "Geez! Where was *that* ball? That looked low." I realized I was probably getting only about half my calls correct.

Finally, after several innings of screwups, I called the coaches together. Laughing at myself, I admitted, "Hey, I wanna let you know this is the first time I've ever been behind a plate and tried to umpire, and you know what? It looked a heck of a lot easier when I was up there in the stands or in the dugout. Just want you to know that I figure I'll have the hang of it by the end of the game!" They laughed ... and I'm pretty sure it was *with* me.

I made it through the rest of the game, and I even got some kudos from the stands as I hustled down the line to judge a close play at third base late in the game. Everyone knew I was making an honest effort in a tough situation.

So what should you take away from my baseball experience? Remember, I was an adult who felt way out of my comfort zone. Heck, I'm a lawyer. Is this a cautionary tale to warn you away from refereeing before you're sure you've mastered everything? Not at all!

In fact, I want to call your attention to something I said at the start of the introduction: It's one thing to know all the rules, and it's another to have a real feel for the game. It takes time and practice to develop that feel.

There are four takeaways from my first experience as a home plate Little League umpire, and I'd like you to keep them in mind as you start down your journey (or your teen's journey) to becoming a soccer referee.

1. It's a lot different *learning how* to referee and *actually refereeing*. There's no better teacher than just getting out there and doing it.

2. Realize that you'll make mistakes. Sometimes, you'll make big mistakes. Don't be too hard on yourself about that, especially in the beginning. Heck, you aren't expected to be any good at all when you first go out there. The parents on the sidelines may say otherwise, but the *real* soccer community knows it and will give you grace.

3. You don't need to internalize every grumble you hear from the sidelines. I knew this was a low-level Little League game, and I knew that the coaches knew it. In this case, their grumbling gave me an opportunity to create smiles.

4. It's okay to tell a referee team or coaches, "I'm a beginner." In fact, I recommend that you tell coaches if this is your first game or season and especially if you're

the only match official. The vast majority of adults are going to applaud your courage to try something new.

Everyone has his or her first game, and we all make mistakes. Even today, over forty-seven years after I picked up the whistle to start refereeing, I get things wrong sometimes … Just ask the coaches!

Every single game, I want to be the best referee on that field for the sake of the players, coaches, and spectators. I want to do my best to make sure the players are safe and the game's fair. I want to uphold the integrity of the game even though it's just a game.

If that's your goal too, this book will help you get to your first game and beyond it with as much confidence and skill as possible. Unfortunately, you'll sometimes be subjecting yourselves to abuse that idiot coaches and parents send your way, but this book will help you deal with that too.

First of all, however, I want to say that you're awesome for putting yourself out there. When you step out onto a soccer field as a referee or assistant referee, you're doing something 99.99 percent of your peers would never think of doing. That's something special.

1

YOU, A TEENAGE
SOCCER REFEREE

I f you're reading this book, I'll bet you've either started to
referee soccer games or are thinking about it. Perhaps a
parent or coach has encouraged you, or maybe a friend has
told you how much money she's making on weekends. Your
local club may have put out an ad. You're probably a player;
most teen soccer referees start out on that "side" of the pitch.

Let me be clear about what this book is and is not. This
book is not about how to register to become a referee because
there are many different leagues, and there are different referee organizations, each with its own process for starting.

This book is not about the Laws of the Game either.
There are many books and videos on that subject, and the
laws change over time anyway. For instance, when I started
refereeing at age sixteen, goalkeepers could pick up the ball,
walk four steps, bounce the ball, and then take four more

steps, and they could basically do that for as long as they wanted.

This is a book about learning how to really love going out there to referee a game. Every referee in the world—from the ones at your five-year-old matches to the World Cup professionals—started this journey in exactly the same way you are: They got the idea that refereeing might be interesting, explored the possibility, studied the Laws of the Game, and finally got out the for the first and sometimes very scary time.

If you've already picked up the whistle or served as an assistant referee, you'll have noticed three things that probably escaped you as a player:

1. There are a lot of Laws of the Game[1] that you never knew existed. There are other things you've always thought of as laws that aren't. For example, there's no law that says a player can't play the ball while on the ground. Similarly, the fact that you "got the ball" doesn't mean that you didn't foul your opponent. And no, "high kick" is not a thing in soccer.

2. The game looks and feels a lot different when you're the one with the whistle, and it's often a lot harder than you thought it was going to be.

3. There are a lot of crazy adults who for some reason want to make your day miserable. Trust me—Most would not dare do what you're doing, and I have recommendations for dealing with them.

---

1 Strange as it may seem, the rules and regulations of soccer have been referred to as "laws" since a document called "The Laws of the Game" was drawn up in 1863.

BECOMING A SOCCER REFEREE IS REALLY COOL!

1.   **When you become a soccer referee, you become an entrepreneur, and that's the greatest thing in the world!** Entrepreneurs are people who develop their particular interests and talents to become better than the average person at those things and then offer their talents to the marketplace. Entrepreneurs create value for the world, and the world pays them for that value. You end up getting paid for something you really like doing. There's nothing better!

2.   **You can work as much or as little as you like.** When I was young, I would often referee three or four games a day and then do that again the next day. Of course, I had to make sure that refereeing didn't interfere with playing soccer or school.

     Later, when I was in law school and working part time in a law office as well as getting ready for our first child, I was still able to enjoy refereeing; I just cut back to a minimal number of games. Today, at age sixty-four, I go out about once or twice a week but never do more than two games a day. I pretty much choose the games I want to do. I have the ultimate freedom of deciding when and where I referee and for the most part what age groups I work. You are in control of how much or how little you work (and earn)!

3.   **If you become good at refereeing, you'll always be in demand.** In many areas of the country, there are far more games than there are referees. As I was putting

the finishing touches on this book in early 2022, there was a critical shortage of referees throughout the country. Now, that doesn't mean that an assignor has to give you *all* the games you want, but it surely puts you in a good position to work hard, develop good relationships with assignors, and get as many games as you want to handle. In short, your opportunities are endless!

4. **You might never have to work at a "real" job while you're young.** Many teenagers work at minimum-wage jobs, but I mean no disrespect there; that's pretty much the only jobs many teenagers can get. But none of those jobs are as fun as refereeing can be. Plus, you'd probably never get to set your own schedule.

   When I was in high school and college, I never worked for anyone else. I made all my spending money refereeing soccer games. In fact, when I got married after my first year of law school, my refereeing money completely paid for my honeymoon! I had put up with a lot of knucklehead adults doing all those games, but I got the last laugh when I was lying on a beach in the Virgin Islands with my beautiful bride (and still my best friend forty years later!).

5. **"Soccer referee" is a cool thing to have on your resume.** I have nine children. I watched them spend a lot of time doing things they really didn't like because they thought, *This will look good on my resume.* There are few people who, once they start refereeing, actually stick with it through high school and college, but

it can be an impressive point on a resume. Were you selected for a regional tournament? Were you identified to go to a referee camp? Do you mentor younger referees? Mention it!

6. **Refereeing teaches leadership skills.** As a referee, you lead others through the game. When you start out, you'll likely be refereeing really young kids. Know which games are the toughest? Yup. All those five-year-old bumblebees huddling around the ball ignoring you and your whistle. This forces you to develop leadership skills and organizational skills and your "voice" on the field.

   As you move up the ladder, you'll find yourself leading twenty-two players, a set of coaches, and your own referee team. This can be really hard at first, but as your confidence grows (and your mindset changes after reading this book!), you'll get better at it.

7. **Networking is real.** It's often true that **who** you know counts for as much or more as **what** you know. These days, when I work with a teenage referee who I think is good and is keenly interested in the game, I make sure to mention this to the assignors and mentors I know.

The real reason I wrote this book for you is simpler and deeper than these seven things however. Yes, sure, you can make money. Officiating can also help you become a better player by showing you the game through the ref's eyes. But I want you to go further. I want to give you a timeless resource for developing mental toughness and a mindset that will help you enjoy your journey as a referee. I want you to look forward to your next game with confidence in your abilities, and I want you to set an example for those crazy adults who would never dare do what you're doing!

You are entering a really cool community, a tribe. Hundreds of thousands of young folks around the world have taken this journey. While some quit after a few years (or even a single game), many more go on to enjoy what I call the best seat in the house for many years and even their lifetimes.

2

ME, A FORMER
TEENAGE REFEREE

I was lucky. I discovered soccer at age nine in Annandale, Virginia, which was a hotbed of youth soccer in the '70s. My friends and I played a lot of soccer. When the weather was good, we'd ride our bikes to a field. When it snowed, we got our parents to drive us to the church parking lot as soon as it was plowed.

I joined my first travel team, the Annandale Cavaliers, when I was twelve. We became U-19 national champions winning U.S. Soccer's McGuire Cup in 1976. Every player on that team went on to play soccer in college, and several went pro. In addition to my travel team, I played the game in high school and captained my team for three years. When I graduated, I played Division 1 soccer on scholarship at William & Mary.

The whole youth soccer scene was different then—lots of volunteer coaches, mostly foreign born. The same went for referees too, who were mostly born outside the United States. Since the parents didn't know much about the rules, I don't remember a lot of yelling at the referees. We figured that since they all spoke with an accent, they must have known what they were doing!

As the game grew in popularity, so did the need for officials. Our coaches encouraged us to give it a try. So when I was sixteen, a couple of my Cavalier teammates and I took a multi-day course taught by a really good guy named Nelson Kobren, over in Maryland. We were the only teenagers. After we passed the test, we got to select our uniforms and other equipment from a table at the back of the room. Mr. Kobren deducted the gear from our pay at the end of our first season. Another table held huge sheets of paper with the schedules of all the games in the area. We could just go through and write our names down on as many games as we wanted! (Remember, email had not yet been invented.)

We became some of the youngest soccer referees in the country, and for a time, we were the only teen referees in Northern Virginia. When games started a week or so later, we had no field training and no video instruction. Heck, there was almost no soccer on TV back then. Earlier that summer, my dad and I had driven several times down to the DC Armory to watch the 1974 World Cup games on "closed circuit TV." (You, on the other hand, have almost unlimited access to quality games on TV. Here's a tip: Spend some time watching how the referees on TV move and signal.)

Mr. Kobren basically threw us out there doing one-man and two-man games. There were no assistant referees (or "linesmen" as they were called) back then. All we knew was what we had learned in the classroom and what we had picked up playing games refereed by guys we were pretty sure knew what they were doing. We just went out and did it.

While all black uniforms were the standard back then, I refereed in some leagues where we wore black and white striped shirts like hockey officials wear. In my early twenties, I was invited to represent Virginia at the U.S. Soccer Youth regionals twice. In college, I also began running refereeing classes for adults who were just being introduced to soccer and wanted to referee.

While playing at William & Mary, I added to my referee money by running the referee program at Tidewater Soccer Club, which meant that I assigned refs to games. Now, this was all during pre-internet and pre-smartphone times. I'd see a buddy on campus and ask, "Can you do the three games on field number three out here on Saturday?" He'd say, "Yes I can," so I'd write that down.

Now, some forty-seven years later, I'm still at it. Know what's cool? There's not a game where I don't learn something new or figure out a new way of approaching situations. The "sport" of soccer refereeing has been really good to me. I've learned a lot and figured out some things that will help you have as much fun with it as I have, and that's why I wrote this book.

MY CAVALIER TEAMMATES AND I WHO IN 1974 BECAME THE FIRST TEENAGE
SOCCER REFEREES IN VIRGINIA. FROM LEFT, ME, JIM PIEDMONT, JOHN BRAY,
CARL STRONG, AND DOUG DUGAN. I WAS THE ONLY ONE TO CONTINUE TO
REFEREE AFTER A FEW YEARS.

3

YOU, THE PARENT OF A TEENAGE SOCCER REFEREE

Congratulations, Mom and Dad, your kiddo has decided she wants to referee soccer games. This may have been at your prompting ("Hey, you need to make some money!"). Or perhaps a coach has encouraged her, or her friends are working as referees. No matter how it happened, know that refereeing is a very cool developmental tool for young people. Your child will have to be organized, disciplined, and confident to put herself out there on the soccer field.

I took the plunge as a teen because my travel coach, Dave Dugan (an Irishman who was also a referee), believed that the more his players understood about the game as a whole, the better the team would be. Coach Dugan, who lead us to a national championship when we were eighteen, was right. If your children are also players, they'll improve their understanding of the game by being involved as referees.

As a longtime referee and a father of nine (four of whom worked as referees), I know what you're thinking. Part of you says it's always really great for your teens to show initiative. The other part of you worries that you'll need to be out there to protect them from other adults because you've seen bad stuff happening on the sidelines.

I'm with you on that.

When I started refereeing at sixteen, my parents didn't attend many of my games. I was the oldest of seven, so my mom and dad had to split their time watching or coaching all of us. They tried to participate in as many of our games as they could.

After my first couple of years as an official, I started refereeing in some of the top adult senior amateur leagues in the Washington, DC, area, and my dad often attended those games. He would drive and park the car in a "safe" part of the parking lot, always pointing out just in case we had to make a quick getaway, which we sometimes did! (In the fall of 1982, I did the British embassy team against an Argentinian team. What fun … Just months after the Falklands war!)

I have good news. You can do many things to help make your child's soccer refereeing career enjoyable. First, if you've never tried it, you might take the course with your son or daughter and then go out and referee with him or her. I promise that you'll learn by doing and your child will really appreciate your hanging with him or her.

Second, you can reinforce the principle of being a "forever learner." Cracking open the book with the Laws of the Game in it should not end on the day of the test. Experienced referees are always going back to make sure they understand the Laws. In fact, as I will show your child in later chapters, having a firm understanding of the Laws of the Game is the best defense against the mental stress of verbal abuse.

Next, go out with them to practice blowing the whistle or waving the flag. These are critical skills that I'll discuss in detail throughout the book.

Go with them to their first game if possible. Your teen is probably a little bit nervous. He or she will likely be assigned as an assistant referee (the one carrying the flag on the sideline or "touch line") and working with someone older and more experienced. Have your teen make it known to the rest of the referee team that this is his or her first day or first season. I always ask young referees, "How long have you been doing this?" because I want to get a good gauge of their experience. Every referee has a first day, so let's not be shy about that. The adult in charge at your teen's first game will probably love the fact that he or she has joined the ranks of match officials.

You should tell your child that you'll just be there to watch, naturally. But if some knucklehead is making life miserable for everyone, **it's your duty to report this incident** to the club or other organizing body for the game. All the adults at a game owe a duty to the youth and to the game itself to **drive referee abuse out.** If you can, discreetly get a video of the abuse.[2] You do not need to approach the knucklehead (I

---

2   Tip of the day: If you get really good video, send it to my friend Brian Barlow at the "Offside" Facebook group.

would, but as a lawyer, I don't advise you to do it). This bears repeating: *We cannot let the abuse of referees and especially young referees persist in this great game.* You can help by accurately reporting misbehavior, so don't be shy about it.

At the end of that first game or even that first season, your teens may or may not want to talk about their performance. Don't press it. Let them know that you're proud of them and that if they'd like to talk about it or get answers to things they don't understand, you can help them do that.

Encourage your child to attend ongoing training and any informal meetings that the local referee groups hold. Many youth clubs offer weekly or biweekly meetings (sometimes over pizza) where young referees can get feedback from more-experienced referees and can ask questions in a safe environment. If you can, sit in. I promise that you'll learn a bunch about soccer too. The referee community is made up of good people.

Last, encourage your teen to join referee groups (with your permission) on social media, and there are many on Facebook. What you'll find is that the referee community is actually much harder on fellow referees than the knuckleheads standing on the sidelines during the game are. We push each other to excellence. We show videos, and what your child will see is that often, very experienced referees come to very different conclusions about the videos they see, and we learn from the debate. We also call each other out on bad habits such as wearing the wrong uniform, failing to run enough in the game, or a lack of knowledge of the laws of the game.

I encountered many challenges as a young referee, but I stuck to it because I had good adult mentors who encouraged me, counseled me, and invited me into their discussions about the game. Nelson Kobren, Peter Johnson, and Walter Durkin were all particularly helpful and encouraging to me.

I enjoy mentoring young referees. If you or your child would ever like to get on a Zoom call to discuss the mindset of refereeing, reach out to me at ben@benglasslaw.com.

AS ADULTS, WE HAVE A DUTY TO PROTECT THE GAME. HERE'S A BANNER I DESIGNED TO PROMOTE SPORTSMANSHIP IN NORTHERN VIRGINIA.

4

YOUR FIRST GAME
AND BEYOND

I've read many books about refereeing soccer games and about sports psychology. In fact, I probably have one of the largest collections of soccer referee biographies and autobiographies in the world. If there is an English-language book out there written by or about a referee, I more than likely own it.

While most people will not have heard of many of those authors, many are very famous in "our" world, and I've learned a lot from reading their life stories. By and large, these books are not about how to call a foul or what signal to use; they're about the work that's required to enjoy life as a soccer referee and the mindsets and strategies they use to overcome criticism and adversity.

For instance, in his memoir *Seeing Red*, Graham Poll wrote about what united most of the referees he has known:

> an enduring love for the game and the desire to support the game. That's why we keep showing up no matter the weather, the behavior of certain participants or spectators, or our own mistakes.

The authors of these books offer a common insight: every referee has his or her first game. For many referees, that first game (like my first baseball umpiring game) was much harder than they thought it would be. At times, they became very discouraged. They each have at least one major error or controversial event they talk about. We all get it wrong sometimes, but sticking with it through adversity produces rewards.

STUDY, STUDY, STUDY

There are several ways to gain experience in anything you do in life, and I will be discussing the importance of practice as well as theory. However, books have a very important place in the development of anyone who wants to achieve excellence.

I am an entrepreneur. I have founded and run two businesses. I have read hundreds and hundreds of books over the years—books about successful businesses and entrepreneurs, books about economics, about philosophy and history, and about management. And books about soccer, of course.

In addition to mastering the Laws of the Game,[3] I recommend that you read some of the biographies and memoirs related to the game. They will tell you a lot about mindset and experience; these guys have seen everything under the sun. Here are some of my key takeaways from years of absorbing professional referees' wisdom.

1. There are some tough crowds out there. You think that travel soccer in your local area is a difficult place to learn? Try Sunday League football in England. It seems that the refs for those games are there just to absorb abuse. This is why Graham Poll stresses a basic love of the game.

2. While making money as a teenager is very cool, over the long run, nobody makes enough money to justify the grief they may sometimes take as referees. You have to find other reasons for continuing to referee. Do things that make you happy. One way to be happy at refereeing (or any job) is to continually work to be really good at it.

3. All "legendary" referees had terrible days. Some of those days are forever preserved on video recordings. (Go to YouTube and search for "worst referee mistakes.") No matter how hard you train, how much experience you have, or how highly rated you are, you're still going to have "one of those days" from time

---

3 I recommend getting a real (paper) copy of the Laws of the Game. Sure, you can get a PDF or download an app, but there's nothing like holding a paper copy, studying it, and highlighting it. Downloads, apps and even prior editions of the rules are at www.theifab.com.

to time. Each one survived his or her worst day ever, however, and many went on to have incredible careers.

4. All successful referees had mentors. They found others who were further along the path than they were, referees they could talk to confidentially, share their experiences with, and learn from. Those mentors and friends were especially valuable on those "worst ever" days. Today, in addition to the referee social medial groups I mentioned above, I have a small group of local referees to share videos, questions, and concerns with.

5. In any given game, at least half the people are likely to be upset by some call you made. Sometimes, players and coaches will blame you for losses; sometimes, bad memories will last for seasons. Sometimes, your "mistake" will cost someone a game. Referee long enough and that will indeed happen. But at the end of the day, your reward will be in knowing that you prepared for your games, worked hard during them, been honest and fair, and reflected after the games on how you could have been better. This is all the game really asks of you.

MASTER THE WHISTLE

Reading to get better about something you like doing is important, and I encourage you to do that as much as you can. However, going out and doing the thing is still the best way to learn a new skill and get confident at it. In refereeing, going out to your first game with the right equipment that you know how to use is important.

Before your first game, get a high-quality whistle and learn how to blow it. I can't stress this enough even though it might sound like crazy advice. Anyone can blow a whistle, right? You'd be surprised at how many young refs I've seen get out there who sound like they aren't confident simply because no one has ever taught them how to make the whistle "talk" for them.

So spend some time practicing. Not in your bedroom, and not in the car on your way to the game! Get out on a field, run back and forth, and just "feel" what it's like to blow a whistle loudly enough to get people's attention. Then practice some different "voices" such as, *That was a bad foul, and I need you to be a little afraid of me* and *Okay, simple foul—Everyone knows it* and the *Tweet Tweet Tweet!* that means, *Okay! Stop! Yellow card coming out! We're taking a break while I write down some information in my notebook.* Again, when you watch your next professional game live or on TV, pay attention to how the referees use their whistles to communicate.

As far as whistles go, the Fox 40 is one of the loudest and most popular. The Valkeen, which costs about $50, is what many professional referees use in big, noisy stadiums. COVID also brought us a selection of electronic whistles to experiment with though some report that electronic whistles "Just aren't the same."

Whatever brand you choose, always keep a spare in your pocket. I once had a whistle (the metal kind with a pea in it) fail three-quarters of the way through a youth game. Talk about a nightmare. Ever since that day, I've carried two whistles in every game.

WEAR TWO WATCHES

Want to show your fellow referees that you "get it"? Wear two watches. If you don't, at some point in your life, one will fail. I remember long ago having the ball hit the arm my watch was on and destroy the watch, a mechanical watch with hands that the ball broke off. I guessed when the game was over rather than asking for help, and I ended up taking well-deserved criticism for that.

The referees and assistant referees doing games on TV are all wearing two watches even though there is a stadium clock and more officials in the video review room who could presumably tell them when time was up!

DRESS LIKE A PRO

Back in the day, I had to get my uniform from Mr. Kobren in Maryland or special order it from England or New York. Today, in the age of internet shopping, there's no excuse for showing up in anything other than the proper shirt, black shorts, regulation socks, and some good (mostly black) shoes. These should be clean (at least at the start of the day) and in good condition.

You'll see that there are many shirt colors to choose from and that some referees you work with will have all of them— yellow, red, green, blue, and black. Just starting out, get your yellow shirt. No need to spend a bunch of money getting shirts you may never need. I haven't worked in black in years, and I've never worn a blue shirt.

When I was coaching youth teams, I hated it when improperly dressed referees would line my team up before the game and do a "uniform inspection." I would have to (quietly) remind them that they were improperly dressed and that if they wanted to "correct" my team, they needed to show up properly dressed themselves. Today, if I'm at a field and see referees who are too lazy to pull their socks up or are running around with shirts not tucked in, I snap a picture and send it off to the assignor. These referees are shocked to pick up their smartphones at the end of a game to see a message from their assignor that reads, "Pull up your socks!"

Showing up on time with a clean, professional appearance sends a signal to everyone at the match. Other referees will get a good first impression of you, and coaches and spectators are more likely to think you know what you're doing and are taking your job seriously. It's worth the time and money to get the right gear and to make sure it's laundered and packed in your bag before each day of matches.

A NOTE FOR PARENTS

This is a great opportunity to teach personal responsibility. If your young referee is running around the house at 8:30 a.m. looking for some socks before his or her 9:00 game, don't help locate the socks. Let him or her suffer the embarrassment of being not properly dressed (and perhaps getting one of those "Where are your socks?" emails from the assignor). I promise this will happen only once!

STUDY LEADS TO CONFIDENCE

The value of being a master of the Laws of the Game came in handy for me in the fall of 1975, near the end of my first full season of refereeing. I was seventeen and doing a "travel" game of ten-year-olds.

One team took a free kick from inside its own penalty area and flubbed it. An attacker swooped in to take the ball and head toward goal. I blew the whistle because at that time, all free kicks from inside one's own penalty area were not considered in play until the ball had left the penalty area.

I knew that because I had studied the Laws of the Game.

The attacker's foreign-born coach went after me viciously. He just knew there was no "rule" that the ball had to leave the penalty area.

He was wrong of course, and I knew it.

The parents on his team joined in because, "How could an American-born seventeen-year-old possibly know more than our foreign-born coach who had played for twenty years?"

Had I not been a hundred percent sure that I had applied the law properly, I would have been crushed and probably would have quit.

Instead, I ended up writing up my first "ejection report," which I include at the back of this book.

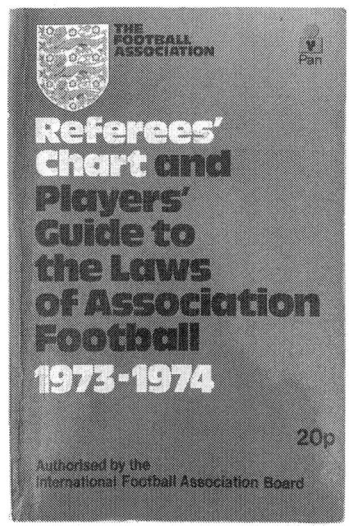

IT WASN'T ALL THAT EASY TO EVEN GET AHOLD OF A RULE BOOK WHEN I FIRST LEARNED TO REFEREE. IN FACT, WE HAD TO ORDER A "REFEREE'S CHART" FROM ENGLAND.

I WAS CURIOUS FROM THE BEGINNING, AND AS SOON AS I FOUND OUT THAT THERE WAS A QUIZ BOOK, I BOUGHT IT AND STUDIED IT OVER AND OVER.

HOW TO PUT YOUR BEST FOOT FORWARD AT EVERY GAME

Prepare for your match no later than the night before the game.

GET YOUR BAG TOGETHER IN ADVANCE.

When you're short on time, your anxiety level increases. If you start putting your referee bag together thirty minutes before you're going to leave for your game, you're bound to forget something. I learned that lesson the hard way.

When I first received my state badge, I was pretty full of myself. One day, I decided to be the cool referee and show up in a pair of crocs planning to switch into my match shoes during the pregame. Unfortunately, I hadn't prepped my bag the day before and had forgotten to put my match shoes in. My first match of a three-match assignment was as an AR, and I ran the line in crocs, which did absolutely nothing for my credibility with the teams or my new crew. They probably thought I had stolen the badge I was wearing.

REVIEW THE RULES OF COMPETITION.

What does the league or tournament want you to do? When are substitutions allowed? How long are the halves? I've found that most of the answers to such questions are easy to find on the Internet. And if I cannot find them, my assignor always knows where they are.

REVIEW THE INFORMATION ON THE TEAMS YOU WILL INTERACT WITH.

There is lots of helpful information on the Internet about teams you will see and even for the youngest ages of travel soccer. Usually starting with U-12 or U-13, competitions record wins and losses. Looking at the standings can provide helpful information as many of these leagues have promotion and relegation.

One of the most helpful sites I have found is GotSoccer. com, which ranks every travel team in America by its state and region and in the nation. Some Canadian youth clubs are included too. You can find out important statistics and information about a team. There are also some leagues that will tell how many yellow and red cards a team or player has accumulated during the season. Perhaps knowing who might be troublemakers is a good thing? *Definitely!*

KNOW THE COACH'S NAME AND THE MANAGER'S NAMES.

It's a good way to introduce yourself and to make a good first impression. I can usually deduce who is the coach by watching a team warm up. (Watching a couple minutes of a team warm-up will also give you a good clue as to the skill level of the teams you're about to officiate.) Many coaches' eyes have widened when I walked up to them and said, "Hi! Are you Coach Dirk? My name's Eric, and I'm going to be your referee today." I was showing them that I was prepared for this match.

FILL OUT YOUR MATCH CARD BEFORE EVERY GAME.

I create my own documents on my computer. I like to include the names and mobile phone numbers of my crewmates in case of emergency.

BE ON TIME.

There's a saying that to be early is to be on time, to be on time is late, and to be late is inexcusable. It definitely applies to referees.

Nothing will ramp up your stress level more than being late to a match. There are several administrative duties you have to perform as a referee before a match begins: the pre-game conference, getting on the same page with your crew, making sure the goals are secured, and the roster check. Skipping any of these can result in confusion, bad calls, bad behavior by the players, or even the risk of physical injury or death to a player!

LOOK THE PART.

Proper attire is important for youth referees because many adults prejudge teen officials unfairly. They say that you get only one chance to make a first impression. When your clothes don't meet the standards set by USSF, the players, coaches, and spectators will think you're not a good referee even before you've blown your whistle for the first time.

WEAR YOUR GEAR CORRECTLY.

This means tucking in your shirt and pulling up your socks. Also, just like the players, referees should not wear any jewelry as they run the same risk of injury if they do.

WATCH YOUR BODY LANGUAGE.

Slouching, yawning, twirling your whistle, or waving your flag like you're signaling the end of the Indianapolis 500—these all send signals that you're bored or distracted. You're getting paid to do a job, so you should give it your best effort. This is a business. If you do a good job, assignors will find out, and you'll receive more job offers and progress to the games that pay more money.

ENJOY THE GAME.

As the referee, you have the best seat in the house. More than once, I've seen an amazing goal, an unreal save, or an exquisite piece of skill and could not stifle the "*Wow!*" that came out of my mouth. Nothing beats calling an advantage that leads directly to a goal. When the losing coach shakes your hand and is genuine when he or she tells you that you did a good job, your match was a tremendous success. So have fun! This is the beautiful game. You are an important part of the match. Competitive soccer cannot occur without a referee. Truly, the game needs you!

—Eric Highsmith

ERIC HIGHSMITH WITH DAUGHTER, KATIE, AGE ELEVEN, JUST AFTER HER FIRST GAME AS A REFEREE. KATIE REMARKED, "WOW! THAT WAS A LOT HARDER THAN IT LOOKED."

KATIE KEPT AT IT AND IN 2017 WAS NAMED NATIONAL FEMALE YOUTH REFEREE OF THE YEAR BY U.S. YOUTH SOCCER.

5

DEALING WITH PLAYERS

As a new official, you will likely serve as center referee in games with players who are younger than you are. As an assistant referee, you may well be assigned games for players your age or a little bit older. As you progress and demonstrate greater expertise, you may even be assigned to referee games with adult players.

Since this book is for teenagers who are beginning their referee journeys, and teenagers will almost always be doing youth games only, I'll leave the "dealing with adult players" for someone else's book. Later, if you decide to continue your career into the adult game, there are plenty of good referee mentors and coaches who can help you get there.

AGES 5–10

In the United States, some leagues start with players as young as four or five years old. The vast majority of those games have no referees at all, which is as it should be because small players just need to get out on the field. Some leagues, partly to give teen officials some low-stakes experience, do assign referees at this level. For games with players up to about ages nine or ten, you may be the only referee assigned to the game. This is how I learned, and it was great experience.

This game is all about fun. Very young players just need someone to lead them on the field. Most have no clue what a goal kick is or how to do a throw-in. They just need someone to keep them (sort of) organized and to restart the game when the ball goes out of bounds. From time to time, you'll also need to keep an eye on one or two rambunctious kids just to make sure no one gets hurt on the field.

The most important officiating ability is leading the players to the next thing to do. This usually involves demonstrating what a kickoff is, showing them how to throw the ball in, and so on. You won't need a honed ability to identify fouls at this level. The important thing is that they have fun in a safe environment. (Of course no matter what the age, that should be the important thing!) Learning to blow the whistle and act like you know what you're doing are the most important skills you need to referee at this age group.

AGES 10–12

When players get to be in the ten- to twelve-year-old range, you will start to see separation between those who will stick with recreational soccer and those who will progress to travel soccer. Generally, children this age are not cynical—They want to have fun, and they respect authority. They're not out there to do anything but play soccer.

Twelve-year-olds in a travel league will likely be watching games on TV and may be slightly more knowledgeable about the laws of the game … or at least think they are. A couple of them may feel that it's okay to challenge the ref—even an old guy like me. Your ability to recognize fouls will be more important, but the critical skill is still organizational. Your ability to authoritatively demonstrate "I'm the line leader" will get you through the day. If you have trouble from anyone in a game involving twelve-year-olds, it's usually a parent or coach, and it is usually minor.

AGES 12–14

The twelve- to fourteen-year-old age group bracket is interesting. Here you will find another split. Some will be developing into really good players and will be invested in the game. They go to specialized camps and may have good coaches to aid in their development. Some are wearing $250 shoes! Others, however, will still be on the recreational track.

With players up to about age fourteen, you can get by correctly determining whether actions are fouls or not. Your player-management skills do not have to be extraordinary, just competent. At every age level, the travel players will likely have greater talent and skill. Some will think they are more expert at the game than they are.

This is a really fun age group to work with. For the most part, they don't go out there intending to cheat or to stomp the other team into the ground. Yes, they commit fouls, but that's usually because they're exuberant, enthusiastic, and a bit clumsy. Most of them won't fake a foul either. The challenge with this group is that they begin to think that they know a lot more about the laws of the game than they actually do. As a teen, your challenge will be your age—you will be only slightly older than these players. Therefore, you must demonstrate mastery of the laws. They will usually know if you don't understand the rules of the game.

Some players, especially those on travel teams, will have high-end game experience and maybe even more than you do. Occasionally, I have seen these players (and their parents) develop a mentality of entitlement: "I play on an elite club team, so I must be right!" I once had a player in this age group who was disagreeing with one of my calls angrily shout at me, "Have you ever played the game?" I stopped the game and began reciting my playing resume starting with a national youth championship and moving on to a college scholarship. I was only about halfway through (and enjoying it) when he said, "Sorry, ref. I get it."

I find that players at this age group tend to be self-conscious in a way younger kids are not. They get more embarrassed when they make mistakes and want to blame somebody else for them. I think sometimes they feel a great deal of pressure from their parents to do well.

There are challenges with older kids in recreational soccer too simply because they're able to run faster and kick farther. In my experience, because their skills don't quite match those of the travel players, it's actually more challenging to work recreational games at the fourteen- to-nineteen age group. With travel players, the ball usually goes where they want it to go, but that's not always the case with recreational games. A referee can't predict quite where the ball may go next. This means more running for you and a bit more chaos to manage. Again, it's usually not intentional or a sign of a bad attitude; it's because they're teenagers and are still learning to control their bodies and their focus.

AGES 14–16

I personally find the fourteen- to sixteen-year-old travel team group the most fun. At this point, you're typically working with players who have decent skills and good coaching. Most of them are still playing for the love of the game. They still tend to respect the ref as long as that person is doing the things this book advises (showing up on time, showing courtesy, working hard, getting most of the decisions correct.) They aren't quite as fast as the sixteen-to-eighteen group, so that's good for older referees like me.

AGES 16–18

The sixteen-to-eighteen-year-old group is in my view the most challenging. They are typically fit, sophisticated about the entire game (high-level skills, team tactics, and the laws of the game), and they want to win. Some have aspirations of playing in college and perhaps professionally. This is the group where you are most likely to find the cynical attitude that results in cheating. They *really* want to win, and when their own skills and team tactics aren't enough, some will try to cheat.

As a teenage referee, if you're assigned to this age group even as the assistant referee, these will likely be your most challenging games. Know that if your assignor puts you in one of these, that's a sign that he or she respects your abilities and wants to challenge you to be even better. Your job is to be prepared for the game, understand that you have been put there to do a job, and let these players (and the adult coaches and spectators) know that you aren't putting up with challenges to your authority on the field.

No matter which age group you deal with, if you find yourself at the end of a hard day thinking about quitting, know that many others have been in your shoes and survived it. In his book *Jack Taylor, World Soccer Referee,* 1974 World Cup Final referee Taylor reflected on his early days as a ref. He recalled this.

> I kept on refereeing at seventeen because it became a challenge. At that age you really like to have your ego inflated. The last thing you want is to keep getting knocked every week. I mean, after having a stinker you would hardly want to go to a Saturday night dance with your girl friend because you would feel

a bit of a failure. I used to go out each week with an attitude that I would show them. Gradually my hide got thicker and thicker…and all of a sudden I found that I was enjoying it. (page 21)

I promise that if you keep showing up after your own "stinker" game, you will also see your skills and resilience growing. You'll enjoy knowing that you are helping kids develop a love of this great game, and you'll develop the kind of thick skin that will serve you well for years to come.

6

DEALING WITH
OLDER REFEREES

In your first matches, you're likely to be assigned as an "assistant referee," the match officials who run up and down the touchline (sideline) and indicate offside, ball in and out of play, and fouls. When I was young, we called these people "linesmen." You'll likely work with referees who are older than you are, especially during your first season. Some will be adults, and others will be older teens.

This is your opportunity to really learn from those with more experience than you. In *Blowing the Whistle, The Psychology of Football Refereeing*, soccer coach and researcher in the world of sports psychology Stuart Carrington reported,

> On average, an official makes 245 decisions per game. 60 of them will be "technical," such as awarding goal kicks or throw-ins when the ball goes out

of play. These are objective judgments. However, 185 decisions are judgments that the official must interpret such as fouls, advantage, or disciplinary action. (page 2)

In short, officials' decisions matter. An experienced ref who understands this will invest the time and effort to help new officials like you to grow.

Good older referees will start by introducing themselves to you and finding out how much experience you have. Be truthful; remember, every ref had his or her first game at some point. They should ask if you have questions and give you a good set of pregame instructions: how the team will work together, what they want you to do when you're not sure whose ball it is for throw-in, whether to wave your flag if there's a foul, what happens if a foul occurs inside the penalty area and is against the defense. In other words, adult referees should welcome you to the job and make sure you feel comfortable.

Not every adult referee makes a great mentor, however. As a young linesman, I could tell that some referees were thinking, *This kid doesn't know much and won't be much help to me. I'm going to do everything myself.* (If you're an adult referee, you should be thinking about how you can do better than that and be a great mentor.)

How should you, a young person, deal with the adult referees at your games? First, show up on time. I say this multiple times throughout the book because I really mean it! Nothing drives me crazier than any official (young or old) showing up to work with me less than twenty minutes before the game.

We have work to do to prepare for the match especially if we've never worked together before. I'm never comfortable with someone who shows up just in time to walk onto the field as the captains are preparing to toss the coin. Instead, I need to get a feel for your experience and comfort level. I need you to ask me questions. This all takes time.

If the official in charge doesn't give a thorough pregame talk, ask, "How can I best help you out today?" This should be a reminder for the referee to go down his or her checklist with you. If the referee doesn't give a helpful answer or says something flippant like "Just do what you were taught" or "Don't screw it up," go down the following checklist of questions with them.

1. When I signal offside and you don't see my flag, what you want me to do?

2. If I see a foul near me, do you want me to signal? What if that foul takes place in the penalty area and is against the defensive team?

3. How do you want me to handle foul throw-ins?

4. If I see something that happens behind your back, how do you want me to get your attention?

5. How will we handle substitutions today?

6. If I'm having problems with a coach or spectator near me, how do you want me to handle that? How should I get your attention?

7. If you award a penalty kick on my end of the field, what will my responsibility be at the taking of the kick?

8. If you want me to watch the goalkeeper's feet, how will I signal to you if there is a violation?

If adult referees shortcut the pregame, you might feel as if you're bothering them by asking so many questions, but you're not. This is their responsibility, and it's the same responsibility you'll have when you become a senior referee. So go down your checklist. These items are important. The best referees—those we all need to model—do this no matter how many games they have officiated.

At halftime and after the game, you and the rest of the referee team should meet to discuss any problems that occurred. If you're curious about a particular call, definitely ask what the referee saw on the play. And always ask, "Is there anything at all that I could have done better today? Do you see anything that I should work on?" A handful of adults may not take their responsibility to mentor seriously and may get impatient with your questions, but they will be in the minority. Most of us care deeply about the game and for the development of young referees. We welcome your questions!

One last thing: If you have an adult referee who doesn't respect you—doesn't give good pregame instructions, never looks your way during the game, and shrugs off your questions—report this to your assignor. Every good assignor knows that adult referees should be mentors and encourage people like you who are brave enough to have entered our family of referees.

BECOMING A REFEREE WILL MAKE YOU A BETTER SOCCER PLAYER. IN 1974, FOUR TEAMMATES AND I TOOK THE REFEREE COURSE. IN 1976, WE WERE THE U-19 CHAMPIONS OF THE COUNTRY.

7

DEALING WITH COACHES

Okay, now on to the hard part—dealing with grown-ups who are yelling at you. What do you do when for the first time in your life an adult who is not your parent, your coach, or a teacher starts yelling at you?

Let's start here.

No adult should ever yell at or belittle a youth referee.

But the sad fact is that some of them do. I too was a teen-age referee at one point, and I remember how hard it could be to deal with an adult who was criticizing my work.

Most adult coaches know that it's not okay to lose their cool with any referee, but in the heat of the moment, they sometimes forget that. I have found that one of four factors usually influences these moments.

First, some do not know the laws of the game as well as they think they do. They watch games on TV. They've heard things about the laws or had things passed down from their own coaches or mentors, but many do not actually have an intimate knowledge of the laws of the game. In fact, most coaches would likely not pass the referee test that you have taken and passed.

I had one recently scream at me, "The ball was moving when the player kicked it!" after a drop ball. A travel coach for a well-respected club team once asked me, "Isn't the restart for a hand-ball an indirect free kick?" On another occasion, a high school coach wanted a "penalty kick" when his forward was fouled forty yards from the goal. Yet another coach thought that I could not award a penalty kick for a foul inside the penalty area if "the ball had already been cleared and was out near midfield."

Second, some coaches do know the laws of the game quite well, but they just saw the incident different from the way you did. Your job involves making decisions in real time from one angle and with only an instant to make the call. Based on their view of the field, some coaches might well be right about what they saw and in challenging your decision of the outcome. From time to time, I see videos of games I have refereed. I appreciate those videos because I learn from them. I'm often surprised at how differently an incident can look from another angle. We can all accept that coaches are occasionally right ... though that doesn't justify them losing their temper.

Third, incidents can happen because coaches can feel stressed and ego gets in the way of their rational brains. They yell at you because their team is not doing as well as they expect them to do (or more likely as well as the parents expect). Stress changes us all.

Last and worst, some coaches yell because they're simply trying to change your next call. It's a nasty psychological tactic.

They may not be able to get you to reverse the call you just made, but they hope they can influence your next call through their bad behavior.

While none of these factors explains away some coaches' misconduct, understanding why they yell can help you prepare to respond. Remember, their actions are not personal; they don't hate you. They probably don't know you. They just hate losing. They get embarrassed when their teams lose. They have to explain why they lost to the parents who paid them to coach. Sometimes, it's just easier to blame the referee.

So, how do you survive the mental stress of getting yelled at by an adult?

The best defense is ironclad knowledge of the laws of the game. Don't get them wrong. Know which fouls restart with an indirect free kick and which restart with a direct free kick. Understand that not every ball that hits a hand or arm means that the game must be stopped. Understand the basic criteria for offside.

Very few people other than referees master these. You must be right on what the rules say. Interpreting what happened on the field is different, but knowing what the rules say is black and white. Don't get that wrong.

This isn't as easy as it may seem—the book containing the laws of the game is rather thick these days—but it is possible. As I said earlier, those who are serious about refereeing purchase an actual hard copy. There's nothing wrong with having an e-book as well, but here's the method of study I recommend.

Get a copy of the laws, and start a journal called "What I Just Learned about the Laws of the Game." In it, write down what you learn (or put it on the device of your choice). I prefer to write it down because there's a ton of science saying that if you learn something and then write down your own understanding of it using pen and paper, you'll actually be able to remember that more than if you just typed it into your device.

Starting with your next referee class—whether it's your first certification or a recertification—highlight and mark up that physical copy of the Laws. Use your journal to write down new things you learn. After every game, go back and review any incidents using the book of the Laws. Write in your journal, "Today, this incident happened in my game: _____" [describe]. When I reviewed it in the book of the Laws, I discovered _____. [Write specifically with the Law says about the incident you are describing.] It might sound like a lot of work, and it is, but I guarantee that if you use these two strategies, you'll become an expert on what the Laws actually say. You will know more than most referees your age and probably most coaches of any age do.

I also recommend taking advantage of all the resources technology has given us. I've compiled a list of some of my favorites at the end of this book. There are many websites and social media groups where referees gather (virtually) to review and comment on videos from actual games. Many of these sites allow us to view incidents from many angles; some even allow us to hear the audio between the referee and the VAR (video assistant referee) team in the booth. Watch enough of these and you'll notice that referees often debate fiercely among themselves about what they just saw three times and in slow motion. Why should things be different in the thick of the game? Different people will naturally come to different conclusions about what they see. You and I, as referees, will often see things differently from the way coaches and players do and even from the way each other does, but that's normal, and it should give you confidence the next time someone yells at you. In many cases, you and the coaches, players, and spectators are simply seeing the same incident from different angles, and angles matter.

We have to learn to accept that we're not always going to be right. The rules of the game account for this; they say that the referee has the final decision on points of fact. Our decisions as to the facts (i.e., what happened) are final. We are the tiebreakers. We are not infallible, but at the end of the day, someone has to make a decision about what happened during a given incident in a game just as players are making decisions about where to run and what to do with the ball and coaches are making decisions about tactics and substitutions. We all have different roles to play.

What do you do with a coach who becomes unreasonable and ventures from his role (coaching) into your role (making decisions about fouls and other incidents of the game)? First, let's define "unreasonable." It's one thing for a coach to call out something like "Hand ball!" as an emotion-driven, brief outburst. We all do that when we watch (or play in) games. But "unreasonable" is when a coach either keeps returning to an incident or has such emotional outbursts about too many incidents during a game. Both must be stopped. This is not the coach's role.

If a coach raises his voice in a brief outburst, that isn't really a problem if you have worked to get in the right position and are focused on the game and simply reached a different conclusion about what it is that everyone saw. If, however, you are not in the right position either because you are lazy or because you don't know what position to be in, the coach may have a valid point. In either case, you can ignore the outburst. As I said, outbursts happen. They are not personal, and when occurring infrequently, they shouldn't cause you any concern.

If a coach persists in telling you how to do your job, makes it personal ("You stink!"), or has emotional outbursts however brief about everything you do, this is a problem. You must stop it in its tracks for the good of the game.

Stopping dissent will be the hardest thing you do as a young referee. (Even most adult referees aren't very good at it.) The person yelling at you is usually going to be an adult coach or spectator, and you have likely not had an adult who was not your coach, teacher, or parent yell at you before.

Before I give you steps for dealing with this, a brief word for the adult referees in the game who may be reading this chapter:

I think experienced referees who blow off consistent misbehavior by saying, "I can take it" or "I have a thick skin" are doing a grave disservice to the game. Professional leagues that allow persistent dissent, which youth coaches and players watch unfold on TV, are not helping the cause. Allowing dissent to grow guarantees that the sport will lose youth referees who aren't hardened to the abuse. Yes, sure, you as an adult referee can "take it," but dissent is not just about you. Officials of all ages must stand up to the bad actors in the game if for no other reason than to protect the teenage referees who will have that team and coach next week.

This goes double for adult referees who are working games with youth assistant referees. You absolutely have to have rabbit ears and pay attention to any grief your young assistants are getting from coaches or spectators. You should be less tolerant of the dissent that your young assistant is getting, and you should *nail* anyone dishing it out. Pay attention to what's going on in your game!

End of rant to the adult referees ...

Here are the steps teenage referees can take for managing adult coaches who start to misbehave.

1. Err on the side of shutting it down. The first time a coach starts to get after your calls in a way that is "unreasonable" (i.e., not just brief emotional outbursts), halt the game at the next natural stoppage (i.e., the ball went out of bounds or you called a foul). Calmly walk to the coach. Walking gives you time to think and to settle your own nerves. Walking to that coach also puts that coach "on display." The spectators know something is going to happen. When you're close enough that he or she plus any assistant coaches and team members can hear you, say in a firm, audible voice, "Coach, I'm going to ask that you leave the refereeing to me today. You're really good at what you do, but let me be the referee." Use those exact words.

   With that slow walk and those calm words, many coaches will shut it down right then and there. Too many adult (but often inexperienced) referees use a moment like this to demonstrate their power over the coach. The wrong way to do this (and I have seen it done this way many times) is for the referee to start yelling at the coach to shut up or to threaten the coach with a yellow card. Far too often, that type of response leads to a clash of egos—and now you have a real power struggle that usually doesn't end well.

When you walk and calmly let them know that you heard them and you remind them very respectfully (and stroking their egos a little) of the role they play and the role you play in the game, you set boundaries that more times than not they will respect. My personality is to do that all with a smile and a *We're in this great game together* mindset because we are in this great game together!

2. If coaches try to argue—"But I'm right!" etc.,—just remind them, "Again, coach, I'm just asking for you to stick to coaching and I will be the referee." You need to be the respectable, calm head in the game.

3. Again, most coaches will back down, but occasionally, you will have one who wants to keep going. At that point, your response should be, "Coach, if I have to come back over to talk to you again, it will be to caution/show you a yellow card."

4. Now if one more word that is not "Sorry, ref" comes out of that coach's mouth, show him the yellow card. You have calmly addressed his concerns three times and he has demonstrated that he wants to win a power struggle. He is wrong. His role is to coach, and yours is to referee. You're not yelling at him for his stupid substitutions or coaching tactics, and he should not be yelling at you for your decisions. Caution him if he persists.

5. Use the same technique if the behavior stops for a while but comes back later in the game. In other words, once you've told a coach, "If I have to come back over here, it will be to caution you," keep your word if necessary.

Here's another reason we must shut down coaches who don't respect the game. This was brought home to me by a lecture that former MLS assistant referee Bill Ditmar gave to the Northern Virginia high school referees in a preseason meeting in 2019. Ditmar said that when a coach is unreasonable, we need to deal with that coach early because otherwise, we send a message to the other coach, the coach who is acting responsibly, that his or her good conduct doesn't matter. I had never heard it put quite that way, but Ditmar is right: We ask coaches to act responsibly, but when they don't and we let them get away with it, we are really saying, "We were only kidding about the 'act responsibly' part."

Now it's possible that your calm talk followed by a yellow card won't shut a coach down entirely. It's rare, but it can happen. When it happens, it usually means that the coach has gotten away with these antics before. Not today. You know what you need to do on the next outburst. It's time for the red card—ejection. It's the end of the game for that coach. When you have to give a red card to a coach, it's not your fault. You're protecting the game. You're also protecting next week's referee.

Whether the incident stops at step 1, step 5, or sending the guilty coach packing to the parking lot, you'll go home after the game and write about this incident in your journal.

(You will also likely have to prepare a written report for your assignor.) In your journal, you want to answer this question: Is there anything at all I could have done to change the outcome? Remember, that question is for you and your mentors to discuss. Keep asking that question throughout your career. That's how we get better at this!

THE VAST MAJORITY OF GAMES I DID AS A TEENAGE REFEREE IN THE '70S WERE ONE-PERSON GAMES. THERE JUST WEREN'T ENOUGH REFEREES TO HAVE THE LUXURY OF "ASSISTANT REFEREES," OR "LINESMAN," AS THEY WERE CALLED AT THE TIME.

8

DEALING WITH PARENTS AND OTHER SPECTATORS

PARENTS!

Go to YouTube and search for "crazy sports parents" or "crazy soccer parents" and you'll find a lot of videos of adults doing stupid things while attending kids' games. Many rational people argue that the youth game would be so much better if we just made the parents stay home (or at least far away from the soccer field). Over the course of your refereeing career, you will get more grief from parents than you'll get from coaches and players combined.

While coaches tend to yell at referees for one of four reasons, with parents, it usually breaks down to two (sometimes a combination of both): 1) They have no clue what the laws of the game really say, or 2) They want their kids to win because somehow, when their kids lose, it becomes a reflection on them.

Good coaches hate these types of parents too. The same jerks who yell at you are the ones trying to coach their kid from the touchline, often contradicting the coach, and sending emails after the game asking why their children didn't get more playing time at the "right position."

Most of these bad apples would never have the guts to put themselves out there on the field as referees. Most couldn't even get up and down the field as you do. They'd crumble the first time anyone yelled at them. They are cowards.

As with coaches, we should not put up with such knuckleheads. I have witnessed games where otherwise rational and decent youth players lost their heads and were ejected from a game because they were influenced by the unsporting behavior of moms and dads on the sidelines.

We know it's going to happen, so how do you manage the situation when parents yell at you? You have two choices: let the coaches handle misbehaving parents (the method most referee instructors recommend) or deal with them directly.[4]

As a teenage referee, you should pick option one. This is the safest way for you to deal with unruly parents. You should not ever have to deal with them directly. Their "role" is only to cheer for their players and teams. If they chose to do something else today, then no, you don't have to put up with them. That's not a part of the game, and the coach should be prepared to deal with it.

---

4   Referee instructors can save the hate mail. I know this is not officially recommended and can be almost impossible to pull off when you're starting out, but I have found that this can be effective as you get more experience.

Here's the procedure.

1. As with a misbehaving coach, call a halt to the game at the next natural stopping point. Walk slowly toward the coach keeping some distance and speaking loudly enough to be heard by the assistant coach. Speak first to the coach, "Coach, I need you to have a word with your parents. Please tell them that we cannot continue unless they agree to behave and stop yelling at me."

    The vast majority of coaches will do exactly what you ask them to do. Again, most are good people who would be as happy as you if problem parents stayed home. (Generally, the children as well would be happier if the loudmouth parents disappeared. Children are confused when their coaches are telling them one thing and their parents are telling them another. They hate it when their parents act like idiots toward referees.) And when coaches speak to the parents in question, generally, they will do what the coach says—stop yelling at you and behave. Problem solved.

2. If the abuse continues, you must stop the game again, identify the parent or parents who must be removed, walk over to the coach, and get the coach to ask those specific parents to leave. Simply tell the coach the game will not be restarted until those parents have left the playing area.

3. If for some reason the coach does not comply, calmly repeat that the game will not restart until the identified adults have been removed. If they continue to ignore your request, you simply end the game. (Remember, referees do not "forfeit" games; they "termi-

nate" games and then make reports to the appropriate authorities—usually their assignors.)

Now to the somewhat controversial second method of dealing with unruly parents. Sometimes, it isn't possible to involve a coach. Usually, he or she is on one side of the field and the parents are seventy-five yards away. The coach may have no clue what is actually going on and might not have any real power over these people.

When parents go outside their roles—cheering for their players and teams—and start to infect your game with their venom, and there's no coach to intervene, you follow the same procedure but speak directly to the parents. (This gets easier when you're older.)

The words to use are: "Sir/Ma'am, we don't do that around here anymore. I'm asking you to let me referee the game. I'm out here doing the best I can." Say it with a big, confident smile.

This is going to work most of the time. Again, what you are doing is letting everyone know that you recognize what's going on (poor behavior on the part of parents) and that this behavior is not going to continue today. You have walked toward the parent and you have spoken calmly.

As with the coaches, the mistake many referees make is to make this into a power struggle. "I've got a referee badge on and you're going to do what I say." Usually, that type of attitude is going to make things worse. Let's be the calm ones in the game. Your mindset should be, *We're all in this together, and the kids want to play.*

While the laws of the game do not actually give you jurisdiction over parents or the authority to "eject" them from a game, I've always thought about it this way: You have the power to not restart the game. If you need to eject a parent, you simply announce that you will not restart the game until that parent has left. You're actually not ejecting anyone. They're ejecting themselves!

In either situation, after the game, write down in your journal what happened. (Again, you'll likely also have to make a report to your assignor.) Why do you think it happened? Is there anything at all you could have done differently to avoid a step such as not restarting a game until an offending parent had left or terminating the game?

Most leagues will come down harshly on teams whose parents cannot behave. Your job is to be the most rational, calm person in the game. Use the opportunity after the game to speak to your mentors or your assignor. Assignors in particular want to know if they have a troublesome group of parents.

Whether you are dealing with a coach or parent, know that all the adults in the game understand that this is hard for young referees. You've likely never had to do anything like this in your life. Adult parents and coaches can be intimidating to teenagers, which is why it is really important that you

1. become a master of the laws of the game,

2. show up on time,

3. be dressed properly,

4. know how to blow your whistle with authority,

5. have mentors you can talk to, and

6. report any misconduct to your assignor.

The assignor knows that if we adults don't shut down the abuse of young referees, the game simply will not have enough referees.

A quick note to the adults who are reading this chapter: For the good of the game, you must stand up for young referees and even those who make big mistakes in games. There is space at an appropriate time after the game for teaching and correction. During play, the more immediate need is for you to lead and stand up against bad conduct by adults in the game. Please do not be that parent who engages in misconduct toward referees or even that parent who stands idly by while a young person is verbally abused. When you do that, you are as guilty as the abuser. Harsh? True.

REFEREEING HAS BROUGHT ME MANY OPPORTUNITIES INCLUDING TALKING ABOUT MY EXPERIENCES AND SHARING THE STAGE WITH NHL AND NBA REFEREES AND MLB UMPIRES AT THE NATIONAL ASSOCIATION OF SPORTS OFFICIALS NATIONAL CONVENTION IN 2018.

CONCLUSION

ERIC HIGHSMITH is a very popular youth, adult, and college referee in our area. We often discuss match incidents, the laws of the game, and of course the subject of this book: mindset.

I once asked Eric what he remembered from his first day of refereeing. How was it? He laughed and admitted, "I wore shin guards in my first match. I thought we were supposed to dress like the players. Nobody said anything." After thinking a minute, he added, "I know that I immediately loved it. I was a practicing attorney at the time, and refereeing played right into my legal training: know the law, learn the facts, and apply the law to the facts."

That's a good summation of how to succeed as a young referee …

… But it isn't really what I hope you'll take away from this book. Of course I want the tips and techniques I and my fellow seasoned referees shared in it to help make your first season fun and rewarding and to set you up for success in the role. More important, however, I hope that you will take away the insight that the experience of officiating soccer can shape a mindset that will benefit you for your whole life. It certainly did for me.

Growing as a referee taught me so many valuable things: how to keep calm and in control when others are losing their cool, how to manage a complex and quickly evolving situation, and how to lead even when others were doubting me. It introduced me to a community I have loved for decades. It laid the early foundation for my growth as a lawyer. It made me a better entrepreneur—I got to put my talents to the test, and as my skills improved, I was able to put my abilities into the marketplace and get paid for it.

Basically, the mindset that soccer refereeing gave me has paid benefits in every part of my life. I believe it can do the same for anyone who gives it a shot and then keeps at it.

If you don't yet see how soccer officiating can offer you the same lifelong gifts, here's a simple breakdown.

1. Keep up. Just as studying the laws and preparing for your matches will help you on the pitch, keeping up your knowledge and skills will help you improve at anything you try.

2. How you show up matters. Just as people respect the properly dressed official who shows up early, how you present yourself in life will influence their first impressions of you in all situations.

3. Bring a pro attitude always and especially if you're getting paid to do a job. Why would you start with anything less?

4. Set boundaries early. Players, coaches, and parents need them during a game. Later in life, your kids will need them as will your employees, colleagues, and friends. If you set them from the get-go, you'll avoid problems.

5. Find mentors. Everyone can benefit from the experience of others who have been there and who have worked hard to develop their expertise.

6. Look for opportunities to gain experience. Study is great, but there's no substitute for getting out there and doing it.

It can be scary to put yourself out there especially as a young person. It will be hard sometimes to subject yourselves to the abuse that idiot adults, coaches, and parents can send your way. But I'll tell you one last time—You're awesome for doing it. You play a critical role in the sport, especially for the kids who are coming up after you and whose love for the game can be cultivated by great refs like you.

—Ben Glass

STILL SPLITTING MY TIME BETWEEN YOUTH AND HIGH SCHOOL GAMES. THIS PHOTO WAS TAKEN BY MY BROTHER DAN, WHO IS BOTH AN EXCELLENT REFEREE AND AN EXCELLENT SPORTS PHOTOGRAPHER. EACH SEASON WE CONVINCEOUR LOCAL ASSIGNOR TO LET US WORK A GAME OR TWO TOGETHER.

'Many Players Dream of Playing in the World Cup' 'I Imagine Refereeing it'

'I Dream Of Being The First American World Cup Ref'

By Paul Harris

If you've ever seen Ben Glass of Annandale, Virginia on the soccer field you'll decide he's one of the most serious students of the game. Bob Vanderwarker of Madison College first noticed Ben almost ten years ago at the Shenandoah Sports Camp.

"I was giving a seminar on the laws of the game to a group of young players. This little red-head in the back of the room kept popping up with some very intelligent questions, a couple that I hadn't even expected. He had an unusual interest in soccer." Vanderwarker, now a linesman for the North American Soccer League and a highly respected college coach, spotted the talent in Glass very early.

"Ben Glass comes from a wonderful soccer family," added Vanderwarker whose games may someday be officiated by Glass.

Glass the player is now enrolled at William and Mary. As a player he is versatile and reliable, and does everything well. The real story of "the red-headed kid in the back of the room" may lie in his refereeing activities and ambitions.

Graham Ramsay, well-known clinician and founder of the Soccer School first brought Glass to *Soccer America*'s attention. "I saw a game last spring that was the best officiated contest I'd seen all year, anywhere, and it was whistled by a teen-ager," mused Ramsay, who seldom exaggerates his soccer stories.

When you meet an accomplished player, one who has played on a national Junior Cup team (Annandale Cavaliers) and he tells you that his real ambition is to referee in the World Cup, you want to learn more. Now 19, Ben has scored an almost perfect score on the Virginia State Referees' test. He is Director

of Referees for the Williamsburg Youth Soccer League and the Peninsula Youth Soccer Association in Virginia. He's read a dozen books on soccer refereeing, and has attended a clinic for NASL referees. Already, he has learned from the best of them, at an age when most players have given up trying to understand the offside. Recently Glass was promoted to linesman in the National Soccer League in Washington.

What motivates a young player, fully eight years before the peak of his game, to take up officiating so seriously?

"I was in the 8th grade and refereed some of my dad's team's scrimmages. I read everything I could get my hands on about the laws of the game." Ringing true with Ben's every word is an intense love for and involvement with soccer, and he knows that his contri-

Photo by Lyle Rosbotham

A TEENAGE REFEREE WITH A BIG GOAL WAS SO RARE IN THE '70S THAT I WAS FEATURED IN *SOCCER AMERICA* MAGAZINE.

Referee's Report

Game: Bowie Vs. Fairfax (65)

Date: 10/25/75

Time: 3:30

Reason for Caution of Bowie Coach:

In the 20th minute of the first half, Fairfax took a free kick from within their own penalty area. The ball was not hit well and a Bowie player touched the ball before it left the area. I blew the whistle and ordered a rekick.

The Bowie coach immediately began to protest vehemently that I was wrong. He said that a free kick does not have to leave the penalty area.

I walked over to him, showed him the yellow card and told him that he was being cautioned for dissent. He told me that it was ridiculous for me to be refereeing when I didn't even know the basic laws of the game. I turned away and resumed the game.

Reason for Ejection of Karl Krueger:

In the 28th minute of the first half, Krueger broke through the Fairfax defence. He had the ball and was followed closely by a Fairfax defender.

Twice, the defender attempted to play the ball but only succeeded in hitting the ankle of the attacker. Both hits occured outside of the penalty area.

After the second attempt, Krueger still had the ball and the defender had dropped back. I shouted for him to play on as by now he was into the penalty area with only the goalkeeper to beat.

MY FIRST SENDING-OFF AND MISCONDUCT WRITTEN REPORT NEAR THE END OF MY FIRST FULL YEAR OF REFEREEING. AS WAS FREQUENTLY THE CASE IN THE '70S, FOREIGN-BORN YOUTH COACHES WERE "SURE" THEY KNEW MORE THAN THE SEVENTEEN-YEAR-OLD AMERICAN.

As it happened, he crossed the ball to the front of the
goal where it was saved by the goalkeeper. Krueger then turned
around, ran at the defender who had been kicking him and deliver-
ed a kick to the back of his legs. The defender turned away
from him and I sent Krueger off for violent conduct.

Additional Incidents of Misconduct:

After play was resumed after the sending off, I was running
up by midfield when I overheard the coach tell Krueger, for all
to hear, "The next time that something like that happens, don't
kick the player, kick the referee."

I took no action here but I think that I could have sent
off the coach for ungentlemanly conduct after a caution. However,
I felt that it may have resulted in the termination of the game
as the Bowie fans were by now very restless. I did not want the
game ended as it was clear the players still wanted to play and
Fairfax was leading at this point, 4:0.

After the game the Bowie coach took my name. He then began
to berate me in front of his players saying:

> "You with a whistle are a joke. It is ridiculous to
> have a referee who does not know the basic laws of the game.
> I can understand having a goalkick come outside the penalty
> area but I have played soccer for twenty years and I know
> that a free kick does not have to leave the area. You
> should be ashamed to referee in front of these kids and not
> know the basic laws of the game!"

Respectfully,

Ben Glass III
MWSRA
256-7237

(cont'd) BEING A SERIOUS STUDENT OF THE LAWS OF THE GAME HELPED
ME STAY CONFIDENT WHEN FOR THE FIRST TIME IN MY LIFE AN ADULT WHO
WAS NOT MY PARENT, TEACHER, OR COACH WAS SCREAMING AT ME.

THE USSF ASSIGNOR ROLE

The referee-assignor interaction is a relationship, and not every USSF assignor is equal. Everything depends on the level of effort an assignor is willing to invest, and while every official should build relationships with multiple assignors, know what to expect so that expectations are met. Each assignor plays four essential roles.

1. THE BROKER

The heart of the assignor's job is to be the matchmaker between soccer leagues, tournaments, clubs, and the referees they rely on to keep the peace. When leagues have scheduled games, they will call the USSF assignor with whom they are under contract and the USSF assignor will sort through all available officials to select those best suited to work those scheduled games, confirm that the officials have accepted those commitments, resolve any game-day problems or issues, and field feedback about how well those matches have proceeded. The assignor has ethical responsibility to treat all officials with fairness and without discrimination on the basis of race, religion, gender, ethnicity, heritage, or age.

2. THE PAYMASTER

The USSF assignor typically bills the leagues or tournaments for the cost of the referees, collects payment, and disburses fees to the officials. There should not be any ambiguity about what each match compensation is going to be. Transactions should always be on the books, adhere to laws regarding taxation and disclosure, and be clear whether they will be rendered in cash, check, or electronic transfer.

3. THE TEACHER

The USSF assignor is a teacher just like you have in school. They are responsible for making sure that each official is certified for the current year laws of the game. When that official sees something that isn't within those laws, assignors help sort out how to handle that situation in the future.

Some USSF assignors send the rules out for each competition to all referees, others post the rules on browsers, and others distribute paper handouts. The referee is responsible for knowing the laws and applying them correctly on the field.

4. THE MECHANIC

The USSF assignor is a mechanic who can help fix problems only if she or he knows what the problems are. They can identify which fields are close to mass transit, know which officials have what experience, and estimate travel times for referees to the fields. The more critical information that is shared with the assignor, the better.

—Jesse Rosenthal

SEVEN DEADLY SINS OF REFEREEING

From the perspective of an experienced USSF Assignor, there are many ways to undercut your potential as a referee. This list shows bright-line, turn-in-your uniform offenses that will make your refereeing career unnecessarily short and brutal for all involved. Avoid them at all costs.

1. NO-SHOW

Few acts destroy the credibility of an official with the same intensity as failing to show up at a soccer field to honor the commitment of an assignment. Beyond the players and their families at the field, ignoring your assignment can force financial penalties on the home team, impose financial penalties on the referee assignor, and ultimately destroy the happiness of everyone who planned to play a soccer game at that field and at that time. Bottom line – being a referee is a professional obligation, a job. When you agree to work, you agree to keep that commitment. Someone who doesn't keep their commitments will be dropped from future assignments – and it's nearly impossible to regain the trust of assignors when an official can't be relied upon to work. Of course, emergencies do happen, which is why you should always have your assignor's phone number with you.

2. CANCELLING AT THE LAST MOMENT

Nearly as bad as a no-show is someone who notifies the assignor that they won't be there 10 minutes before kickoff.

With little time to find an alternative, it is likely that a replacement official cannot be found. It is the responsibility of each official to manage their family obligations, transportation to the field, and their professional equipment.

3. SHOPPING

This is the unethical practice of requesting overlapping assignments from multiple assignors, choosing the most attractive one (more money, closer to home, preferred age group, etc.), and backing out on the others. When an assignor selects an official, dozens of factors go into that assignment. If an official is shopping and drops out for something better, all of that work is wasted. Just as the official wouldn't want the assignor to look for a "better" official after accepting an assignment, the official needs to honor his/her commitment.

4. IDIOCY

Think before you act, and don't do these things:

- Going to the field without your referee uniform or equipment

- Insulting your fellow officials or the players

- Telling racist/sexist/ethnic/disability jokes or hurtful statements that demean others – or tolerating/enabling those who do.

- Accept an assignment that you don't plan to keep.

- Keeping your referee obligations secret from your family.

- Taking other people's equipment, wallets, cash.
- Making up rumors about other people.

5. FINGER POINTING

When a problem arises, tell the truth and accept the consequences of your own actions. Blaming other people for your mistakes – even when there may be justification or causality – looks cowardly and is almost always unnecessary.

6. LYING

Always tell the truth. About little things, about big things. It is difficult to regain your credibility and trustworthiness when you are caught in a lie, and will lead others to question the integrity of your decision-making on the field as well as off.

7. OVERCOMMITTING

Know what your body and mind can do – and not what you might do if you were wearing a cape and had magical powers. What happens if you are injured in the morning? How would you explain to the afternoon match players that they are missing their referee because you were circumventing the rules of their assignor that limit the number of games that you can work in a day? Additionally, studies have shown that there are only so many minutes where a human can pay attention without getting mentally fatigued. In soccer, that threshold starts to show up after your fourth game – when your brain can't keep up with which goal the red team is shooting at and you accidentally signal a goal kick instead of a corner kick.

—Jesse Rosenthal

WHAT DOES SUCCESS LOOK LIKE?

PAYDAY

For many referees, getting paid for your work is not the entire sum of happiness, but is a huge contributor. Refereeing <u>is</u> a job, and being paid <u>is</u> a milestone. Well done. Whether the proceeds go towards college savings, spending money, the household bank, or new equipment, you DID this – with the support of your family and friends, sometimes even teammates. Make sure you thank them, too, especially if they assisted with transportation to the field or even served as patient listeners when a game was rougher than anyone expected or wanted.

BECOMING A BETTER REFEREE

Many sources of information come your way as a referee, and some are more important than others. Mastering a positioning tactic for getting out of the way, sharpening your understanding of how to execute penalty kicks or kicks from the mark by watching an experienced colleague do it correctly – the trick is listening and watching so that you can do it better. Sooner or later, you'll be sharing the same wisdom with your newer friends and colleagues; we all pay it forward. When you keep the hunger for learning and performance on the field, hopefully you will find recognition from the assignor, the league, or even a higher level of competition – any of whom are able to open the doors to tougher competitions and challenges. Asking for feedback from those same colleagues is the key to improvement; no one has ever had a perfect game, not even the FIFA referees we see on the World Cup or top professional leagues.

BECOMING A BETTER PLAYER

Having your eyes open on the soccer field gives a new perspective on tactics, either team or individual, that may help you elevate your own soccer game. Finding the key players for each team and watching how they go about winning is one of the hidden benefits from being on the touchline or in the center circle … and best of all, you're PAID for being there.

MAKING NEW FRIENDS

Keeping the communication lines open makes it easy to win new friends – but be careful to win their friendship for your diligence, not because you are doing a "favor" for one team. Referee colleagues are a tremendous source of friendship and mentoring, many who have walked the same path you have now started, and are eager to invest in your success. Players and coaches frequently recognize the hard work you completed so that their game was fair, fun, and competitive. They may cheerfully share their appreciation. Take it at face value.

—Jesse Rosenthal

WHEN TO MOVE ON

Every referee should understand that there are many referee assignors out there. Some focus on recreational matches for a single club or organization, others handle adult matches, others work on youth travel, and some support professional and FIFA assignments.

As a referee, you have the choice to work for any assignor. A relationship can deteriorate for real reasons or perceived issues. It is a good idea to have a direct conversation with the assignor if you're unhappy so you can address concerns before they become problems, but it also can be time to move on.

What are the signs that it is time to end a relationship with an assignor?

WHEN THEY THINK THEY OWN YOUR TIME AND LABOR.

Slavery is illegal. No one assignor owns your time until you have *accepted* that assignment. You can cold-call a new assignor, ask a referee colleague to make a referral, or stop by a field with players you have never seen before and ask in which league they're playing. It's your responsibility to follow up and make sure you're fulfilling your obligations for each match without shopping assignments against multiple assignors.

WHEN IT ISN'T FUN.

There are times when you will come home from refereeing and think, *Why did I agree to work that match?* Maybe there is a routine that gets old and you're seeing the same players and coaches over and over. Maybe you're looking for a new challenge or to work with more-experienced colleagues. These good opportunities to discuss your feelings with the assignor to see what can be improved. If you're not having fun, the players will figure it out, and they may not be sympathetic. Keep your mind fresh and open, and good things will be possible.

Try to avoid commitments beyond a month at a time. As helpful as it can be to lock in your schedule every week, it's hard to anticipate your future growth as an official or to rule out new opportunities. While it's a spectacularly awful and unethical idea to return assignments after you've made a commitment to work them, keeping your options open is one effective way to mitigate against a routine becoming dull.

THEY CONFUSE FAIRNESS AND EQUALITY.

An assignor should not show blatant favoritism. That said, it can be tempting to compare schedules and opportunities with your friends and notice an apparent inequity in the caliber or quantity of assignments. Don't assume automatically that unfairness is the culprit as each official learns at his or her own pace. They start from a deeper base of soccer knowledge because of their team training and coaching, and that helps them apply that advantage or take better positions on the soccer field for proximity and visibility.

Just as it is unfair for an assignor to prefer one referee over another when they are evenly matched, it is unfair to accuse the assignor of a bias or prejudice if there may be an alternative explanation. When looking at fairness, I would ask, "Does each official have the same chance to work? Are they being paid the same fees per match as other officials in the same league, age group, or competition level? Are they each willing to pursue opportunities in different roles and competition levels? Are they approaching every match with a positive attitude?"

—Jesse Rosenthal

BIOGRAPHIES

ERIC HIGHSMITH began playing soccer in the first grade, in 1972. He loved the sport because he could be competitive despite being the shortest kid on the pitch.

The Seattle Sounders arrived in 1974, and he was fortunate to see Pelé play when the New York Cosmos came to town. His boyhood friend and teammate, Adrian Hanauer, grew up to become the managing partner and majority owner of the Sounders.

He drifted away from the sport as a teen, but when he became a father, he made sure to sign up Katie, his oldest daughter, for the local AYSO league. He also joined the team as an assistant coach.

At one of Katie's first matches, when the referee tried to restart play after a goal with a goal kick, he told the head coach, "I could do so much better than this guy." The coach replied, "So why don't you?"

Highsmith signed up for a referee class the next season. Since then, he has served as a referee and referee instructor for almost twenty years now.

JESSE ROSENTHAL is a USSF assignor in the Washington, DC, area. High school, college club, USSF, corporate picnics—he has assigned them all. He's been responsible for thousands of matches a year for more than fifteen and in a hundred-mile radius.

A former USSF associate referee instructor, he has taught both entry-level new referee classes and referee recertification classes. His rules of the road are simple.

- Tell me your name so I'll know with whom I am communicating.

- Tell the truth and I will do the same.

- Speak with respect and I will return it.

RESOURCES FOR YOUNG REFEREES

YOUTUBE CHANNELS TO FOLLOW

MinnsotaSRC—The YouTube home of the Minnesota State Referee Committee

Inside Video Review (from PRO)

YOUTUBE VIDEOS TO HUNT DOWN AND WATCH

These videos will inspire you, and you should be able to find them by typing these titles into the YouTube search bar:

Listening in on the Tough Calls a FIFA Referee Must Make

Ref Cams, VAR, & Managing the Game: Inside the Mind of a Professional Soccer Referee

Behind the Whistle: US Soccer Referee Nick Balcer at the DA Summer Showcase & Playoffs

The Referee 1/2

The Referee 2/2

Behind the Scenes with a Top Referee

Referees are AWESOME

Mic'd up/An exclusive look at a referee's perspective of an A-League game

Match Day with Referee Neil Doyle

FACEBOOK GROUPS TO JOIN OR FOLLOW

Offside

Ref Next

Soccer Referee Society

Referee's Discussion Group

Referee and Soccer Bits

WEBSITES OF INTEREST

RefNext.org

IFAB.org

RefereeStore.com

ProReferees.com

FIFA.com

USYouthSoccer.org

BOOKS

Many of these books are out of print, but they do show up on eBay from time to time.

Seeing Red, Graham Poll

Jack Taylor—World Soccer Referee, Jack Taylor with David Jones

One Night at the Palace—A Referee's Story, Allen Wilkie with George Miller

Give a Little Whistle, Gordon Hill and Jason Thomas

Whose Side Are You on, Ref?, Norman Burtenshaw

Lynch the Ref, Kevin M. Lynch

Collina, the Rules of the Game, Pierluigi Collina

Blowing the Whistle: The Psychology of Football Refereeing, Stuart Carrington

Elite Soccer Referees Officiating in the Premier League, La Liga and Serie A, Tom Webb

The Final Whistle, Arthur Ellis

Knight of the Whistle, Phil Dennett and Jeremy Gambrill

Soccer Refereeing, Denis Hawell

Added Time, Mark Halsey

By the Book, Clive Thomas

Quest for a Cup, Toros Kibritjian

In the Eye of the Whistle: The Refereeing of the 1990 World Cup, edited by David J. Ross

The Man in the Middle, Mervyn Griffiths

Refereeing Round the World, Arthur E. Ellis

Association Football Match Control, Stanley Lover

In the Eye of the Whistle: Refereeing at the 1986 World Cup, edited by Davis Ross

Oh Ref, Pat Partridge and John Gibson

Who's the B*s*a*D in the Black? Confessions of a Premiership Referee, Jeff Winter

The Man in Black, Gordon Thomson

The Inner Game of Soccer, Eric Sellin

Soccer Refereeing, Denis Hawell

Hackett's Law, Keith Hackett

In Search of Fair Play: The Soccer Writings of Emerson Mathurin, D. C. Emerson Mathurin

For the Good of the Game—Modern Techniques and Practical Wisdom for Today's Soccer Referee, Robert Evans and Edward Bellion

Referee! A Year in the Life of David Elleray, David Elleray

Soccer Refereeing: A Personal View, Jack Taylor

WA